# Whoopies!

# Whoopies!

Fabulous Mix-and-Match Recipes for Whoopie Pies

Susanna Tee

STERLING

New York / London
**www.sterlingpublishing.com**

# Contents

# Introduction

*A cupcake please... No, make that a whoopie!*

So, what's the secret? How does a delicious delicacy that has only been sampled by the chosen few suddenly become a global trend? Certainly, in the case of the whoopie or whoopie pie, that is exactly what seems to have happened. One moment, cupcakes had the big city bakery shelves all to themselves; and the next, the whoopie pie had turned up like a forgotten country cousin and muscled in on the action. Perhaps those regions where whoopies have long been a traditional treat decided they had kept their secret long enough. Maybe the whoopie just needed to find its way to the fashionable bakeries both nationally and internationally for word to spread. What is not in question is that everywhere from New York's Magnolia Bakery to Harrod's in London, and many bakeries sandwiched in-between, the whoopie is winning new fans.

The recipes in *Whoopies!* capture some of those things that might lie behind the whoopie's success. There are simple options for the basic whoopie that might be considered more manly than your average cupcake. Then there is a dazzling variety of cakes and fillings, so that you can discover the true versatility of the whoopie. For whoopies as fancy as the prettiest cupcake, you will discover how to add sugar glaze or roll your whoopie in delicious decorations. Children will love to help decorate them, and to clean the bowl. The recipes are grouped by the four seasons so that you can enjoy the freshest local ingredients when choosing which ones to make next. There are also ideas for presenting your whoopies for special occasions, and templates for gift boxes. So, what's the secret of the whoopie's success? Read on, and find out.

# Whoopie Doo

# A Short History of Whoopies

*A whoopie pie, a whoopie cake, or do you call it a whoopie cookie?*

Not only is the name of the whoopie unclear, but its origins are also uncertain. The whoopie would probably be declared the official dessert of Maine if such a thing existed, but Boston and Pennsylvania also claim the honor of being its birthplace.

There are Mainers who will testify that they were weaned on whoopies. One theory is that whoopies were introduced to Maine when a woman working in a commercial bakery baked some leftover cake batter instead of wasting it, and put it together with some extra filling. From this, the whoopie was born.

The Boston claim is through a recipe leaflet, first published in 1930 by the Durkee Mower Company, called The Yummy Book. The company is the manufacturer of Marshmallow Fluff®, which is used as a whoopie filling. The Yummy Book is still in print and has been updated many times, although a recipe for whoopies didn't appear in the publication until the 1970s.

Food historians, however, believe that it was the Amish women living in the Pennsylvania region who created the whoopie. Whoopies are certainly part of their culture and they are sold at all Amish markets, farmers markets, roadside stands offering baked goods, gas stations, and convenience stores. One view is that the origins of the whoopie lie in medieval Germany, and when the Amish settled in Pennsylvania in the nineteenth century, they brought the whoopie with them. Another unproven notion is that Amish women baked leftover cake batter and put the resulting pies in their husband's and children's lunch boxes. On opening and finding the goodies, the latter shouted "Whoopie!" for joy.

Whatever its name or origins, the whoopie is the perfect easy-to make, fun-to-eat treat for any occasion. This cookbook has a year's worth of sweet recipes sandwiched between its covers, and as the song writer Gus Kahn wrote for the 1928 Broadway musical *Whoopee!*:

*Another season, another reason, for makin' whoopee*

Or, in this case, whoopies! So simply delve into these pages to find a collection of delectable recipes. Whoopie!

Below: **Amish workers carrying their lunch out to the fields seem to suspect that the man on the right has a whoopie packed in his lunch box.**

# Equipment & Ingredients

A large bowl, a freestanding mixer, or a handheld electric mixer, several large baking sheets, parchment paper, a wooden spoon, a tablespoon, palette knife, strainer, and wire rack are all you need. A whoopie pan, an ice-cream scoop, and a pastry bag with a large star tip are useful.

The whoopies can be baked on large baking sheets (keeping the batter well apart to allow for spreading). I have found that the sheets worked best when lined with parchment paper instead of being greased. Alternatively, you can use a whoopie pan, which has 12 shallow wells, and these should be greased.

Spooning the whoopie batter onto the baking sheets or into the wells of the pan with a tablespoon, using a finger to slide it off the spoon, is the traditional way, but using an ice-cream scoop creates uniform shapes. Choose one that measures 2 inches/5 cm in diameter.

A strainer is necessary to incorporate the dry ingredients evenly into the mixture, and a wire rack is needed to let the whoopies cool without becoming soggy underneath. Once baked, the whoopies need to be left for only a minute or two on the sheets or in the whoopie pan to let them settle before transferring them to a wire rack.

NOTES
- This book uses **US** standard measurements and metric. Follow the same units of measurements throughout; do not mix US standard measurements and metric.
- All spoon measurements are level. Teaspoons are assumed to be 5 ml and tablespoons 15 ml.
- Recipes using raw egg whites should be avoided by infants, the elderly, pregnant women, convalescents, and anyone with a chronic illness.
- Unless otherwise stated, milk is assumed to be whole, eggs are extra large, and individual fruits are medium.
- Pregnant and breast-feeding women are advised to avoid eating peanuts and peanut products.

The basic ingredients for whoopies are flour, a raising agent, salt, sugar, egg, a milk product (usually buttermilk) or milk, a fat, and a flavoring, very often vanilla, which, in fact, brings out the flavor in chocolate whoopies. Traditionalists consider that whoopies should only be chocolate flavored, but these days flavorings vary.

The best-risen whoopies are those that use all-purpose flour and baking powder, but whoopies are traditionally baked with buttermilk, which nowadays replaces naturally sour milk, and this acid ingredient needs baking soda (an alkali) to balance the acid to alkali ratio.

Granulated sugar is also a traditional ingredient, but superfine sugar can be used instead. Brown sugar, either light or dark, is equally suitable, adding color and flavor to the whoopies and making them slightly moister.

Extra large eggs have been used in the recipes and ideally should be removed from the refrigerator before using to let them come to room temperature. This prevents the mixture from curdling, but it isn't essential so don't worry if you forget.

The recipes in this book use butter, because most households will already have it in the refrigerator. However, there is no reason why you can't replace all or part of the butter with vegetable shortening if you prefer. Vegetable oil is also sometimes used.

Traditional fillings include Marshmallow Fluff®, the original commercially produced marshmallow crème. Other marshmallow crèmes have a thinner consistency and you may need to add a little more sugar to thicken them.

# Hints for Perfect Whoopies

While making whoopies is pretty simple and you're probably debating which recipe to make first, take a few moments to read through these few secrets that I have discovered on my quest to bake the perfect whoopie.

- Before you do anything, preheat the oven.
- Measure the ingredients accurately and use the correct standard measuring spoons.
- Don't overmix the batter; stir gently until the ingredients are just combined. There are several reasons for this: overmixing will cause the batter to peak in the oven and have a tight, compact texture, resulting in a tough whoopie without that melt-in-the-mouth quality.

- It's fine to let the batter rest for 5 minutes on the baking sheets or in the pan before baking, but don't leave it any longer because, in the case of baking powder, once liquid has been added to it, it will start to activate.
- Try to resist the temptation to open the oven door during baking, but be vigilant toward the end of the cooking time, because the whoopies can change color in a minute or two.
- Oven temperatures vary and we tend to know our own ovens. I suggest that if you are baking several sheets of whoopies at once, instead of rotating them during cooking, it is best to bake the top sheet for about 10 minutes, remove it from the oven, and then move the bottom sheet up a shelf and bake for an extra 2–3 minutes. If you have a convection oven, reduce the oven temperature by 25°F, or follow the manufacturer's instructions.

# Filling Whoopies

When the whoopies are cold, match each whoopie half with its closest partner in size. The filling can then be spread onto the whoopies with a palette knife or knife, but it looks more attractive when swirled on using a pastry bag fitted with a large star tip.

The best way to fill a pastry bag is to put a large star tip in the end and then stand the bag in a pitcher or tall glass and fold back the top of the bag. Spoon the filling into the bag and turn down the top. Only fill it halfway up the bag, because otherwise when you pipe the mixture, it will come out the wrong end.

To pipe the mixture, put the tip of the filled bag close to the whoopie and, holding the bag in one hand and supporting it underneath with your other hand, squeeze the bag firmly to push out the frosting. When you have finished, lift the bag sharply off the cake and you will have a beautifully filled whoopie.

# How to Store Whoopies

As a batch of baked whoopies usually makes about 12, you may want to know how to store them. They can be stored in an airtight container in a single layer or stacked, with the layers separated with parchment paper. Alternatively, wrap them individually in plastic wrap. They will keep at room temperature for up to three days, if any should happen not to have been eaten before then.

Whoopies can also be packed in an airtight freezer container or wrapped individually, undecorated, and stored in the freezer. Thaw at room temperature for 2–3 hours before serving.

# How to Eat a Whoopie

When it comes to eating, you will be aware that some of the generous filling is lost out of the sides. When this happens, open it, collect up the filling that has oozed out with a finger, put it back onto the bottom half, and then recreate the whoopie—only to do it all over again a few bites later. This is the correct way to eat a whoopie.

# Spring

# Classic Whoopies

*Makes 12*

½ cup (1 stick) butter,
 softened, plus extra
 for greasing
1 cup dark brown sugar
1 tsp vanilla extract
1 extra large egg
2 cups all-purpose flour
½ cup unsweetened cocoa
1¼ tsp baking soda
pinch of salt
1 cup buttermilk

*Filling*
Homemade Marshmallow
 Crème (see page 75)
 or Classic Marshmallow
 Filling (see page 73)

This is the traditional whoopie recipe, featuring a chocolate cake batter similar to that other great classic, the rich, dark devil's food cake, filled with Homemade Marshmallow Crème.

1 Preheat the oven to 375°F/190°C. Line 3–4 large baking sheets with parchment paper or grease the wells of a whoopie pan.

2 Put the butter, sugar, and vanilla extract in an electric mixer bowl, or use a large mixing bowl and a handheld electric mixer, and beat together until light and fluffy. Beat in the egg.

3 Sift the flour, cocoa, baking soda, and salt into the bowl and stir together. Add the buttermilk and stir until combined.

4 Using a level 2-inch/5-cm ice-cream scoop or heaping tablespoon, make 24 halves. To make each half, put the batter onto the prepared sheets in 2-inch/5-cm-diameter rounds about 1¼ inches/3 cm high, or into the prepared pan. If you are using baking sheets, leave at least 3 inches/7.5 cm between each round to allow room for spreading.

5 Bake in the oven for 10–12 minutes, until firm to the touch. Transfer to a wire rack and let cool.

6 When the whoopies are cold, match each whoopie half with its closest partner in size. Spreading with a palette knife or using a pastry bag fitted with a large star tip, cover the flat side of one whoopie half of each pair generously with the filling. Top each with its matching half, flat-side down, and press gently together.

## Plus One: Ice Cool

Wrap each filled whoopie individually in plastic wrap and freeze. To serve, let soften slightly at room temperature for about 30 minutes before eating like an ice-cream sandwich. Alternatively, fill the whoopies with ice cream and serve immediately.

# Red Velvet Whoopies

*Makes 10*

½ cup buttermilk
½ tsp vanilla extract
½ tsp red paste food coloring
1½ tsp distilled white vinegar
½ cup (1 stick) butter,
  softened, plus extra
  for greasing
1 cup granulated sugar
1 extra large egg
2 cups all-purpose flour
1 tbsp unsweetened cocoa
½ tsp baking soda
pinch of salt

*Filling*
**Cream Cheese Filling**
  (see page 76)

This whoopie is based on the famous red velvet cake. The color is from red food coloring, although grated beet was traditionally used. During the 1920s, it was a signature cake at the Waldorf-Astoria Hotel in New York and, according to legend, when a guest asked for the recipe, she was billed such an exorbitant amount that she spread the recipe via a chain letter.

1 Preheat the oven to 375°F/190°C. Line 3–4 large baking sheets with parchment paper or grease the wells of a whoopie pan.

2 Put the buttermilk, vanilla extract, red food coloring, and vinegar in a bowl and stir together.

3 Put the butter and sugar in an electric mixer bowl, or use a large mixing bowl and a handheld electric mixer, and beat together until light and fluffy. Beat in the egg.

4 Sift the flour, cocoa, baking soda, and salt into the bowl and stir together. Add the buttermilk mixture and stir until combined.

5 Using a level 2-inch/5-cm ice-cream scoop or heaping tablespoon, make 20 halves. To make each half, put the batter onto the prepared sheets in 2-inch/5-cm-diameter rounds about 1¼ inches/3 cm high, or into the prepared pan. If you are using baking sheets, leave at least 3 inches/7.5 cm between each round to allow room for spreading.

6 Bake in the oven for 10–12 minutes, until firm to the touch. Transfer to a wire rack and let cool.

7 When the whoopies are cold, match each whoopie half with its closest partner in size. Spreading with a palette knife or using a pastry bag fitted with a large star tip, cover the flat side of one whoopie half of each pair generously with the filling. Top each with its matching half, flat-side down, and press gently together.

## Plus One: Black & White Red Velvet

Sift 1¾ cups confectioners' sugar into a bowl. Add 5–6 teaspoons hot water and stir until smooth and thick. Transfer half the mixture to another bowl. Add to the second bowl 3 tablespoons cocoa and mix, adding water if necessary, until thick. Coat one half of each filled whoopie with white frosting and the other half with chocolate. Let set.

# Carrot Cake Whoopies

*Makes 12*

2 carrots, 8 oz/225 g total
  weight
½ cup walnuts or pecans
½ cup (1 stick) butter,
  softened, plus extra
  for greasing
1 cup light brown sugar
1 tsp vanilla extract
1 extra large egg
2⅓ cups all-purpose flour
1 tsp baking powder
1 tsp baking soda
1 tsp ground cinnamon
½ tsp ground ginger
½ tsp grated nutmeg
pinch of salt
¼ cup orange juice

*Filling*
**Cream Cheese Filling**
  (see page 76)

**Grated carrot adds sweetness to these whoopies, which are sandwiched together with Cream Cheese Filling in a much loved pairing. Serve them any time, but they are especially appropriate for Easter, carrots being the Easter bunny's favorite food.**

1 Preheat the oven to 375°F/190°C. Line 3–4 large baking sheets with parchment paper or grease the wells of a whoopie pan.

2 Grate the carrots and finely chop the nuts.

3 Put the butter, sugar, and vanilla extract in an electric mixer bowl, or use a large mixing bowl and a handheld electric mixer, and beat together until light and fluffy. Beat in the egg.

4 Sift the flour, baking powder, baking soda, cinnamon, ginger, nutmeg, and salt into the bowl and stir together until combined. Fold in the nuts, carrots, and orange juice.

5 Using a level 2-inch/5-cm ice-cream scoop or heaping tablespoon, make 24 halves. To make each half, put the batter onto the prepared sheets in 2-inch/5-cm-diameter rounds about 1¼ inches/3 cm high, or into the prepared pan. If you are using baking sheets, leave at least 3 inches/7.5 cm between each round to allow room for spreading.

6 Bake in the oven for 10–12 minutes, until firm to the touch. Transfer to a wire rack and let cool.

7 When the whoopies are cold, match each whoopie half with its closest partner in size. Spreading with a palette knife or using a pastry bag fitted with a large star tip, cover the flat side of one whoopie half of each pair generously with the filling. Top each with its matching half, flat-side down, and press gently together.

## Plus One: Carrot & Chocolate Chip

Instead of the walnuts or pecans, use the same quantity of semisweet chocolate chips.

# Gluten-Free Chocolate Whoopies

*Makes 12*

½ cup (1 stick) butter, softened, plus extra for greasing
1 cup dark brown sugar
1 extra large egg
2 cups gluten-free all-purpose flour
½ cup unsweetened cocoa
1½ tsp gluten-free baking powder
½ tsp baking soda
pinch of salt
1 cup buttermilk

*Filling*
**Homemade Marshmallow Crème (see page 75) or Classic Marshmallow Filling (see page 73)**

No one needs to feel left out when it comes to enjoying whoopies, even those who have an intolerance to gluten. So if you or a friend can't eat gluten, you can still safely tuck into these.

1 Preheat the oven to 375°F/190°C. Line 3–4 large baking sheets with parchment paper or grease the wells of a whoopie pan.

2 Put the butter and sugar in an electric mixer bowl, or use a large mixing bowl and a handheld electric mixer, and beat together until light and fluffy. Beat in the egg.

3 Sift the flour, cocoa, baking powder, baking soda, and salt into the bowl and stir together. Add the buttermilk and stir until combined.

4 Using a level 2-inch/5-cm ice-cream scoop or heaping tablespoon, make 24 halves. To make each half, put the batter onto the prepared sheets in 2-inch/5-cm-diameter rounds about 1¼ inches/3 cm high, or into the prepared pan. If you are using baking sheets, leave at least 3 inches/7.5 cm between each round to allow room for spreading.

5 Bake in the oven for 10–12 minutes, until firm to the touch. Transfer to a wire rack and let cool.

6 When the whoopies are cold, match each whoopie half with its closest partner in size. Spreading with a palette knife or using a pastry bag fitted with a large star tip, cover the flat side of one whoopie half of each pair generously with the filling. Top each with its matching half, flat-side down, and press gently together.

## Plus One: Gluten-Free Cinnamon & Yogurt

Omit the cocoa and increase the flour to 2⅓ cups. Sift 1 teaspoon ground cinnamon in with the dry ingredients in Step 3 and use 1 cup plain yogurt in place of the buttermilk.

# Peanut Butter Whoopies

*Makes 12*

4 tbsp butter, softened,
    plus extra for greasing
1 cup light brown sugar
5 tbsp smooth or chunky
    peanut butter
1 tsp vanilla extract
1 extra large egg
2⅓ cups all-purpose flour
1 tsp baking soda
pinch of salt
1 cup buttermilk

*Filling*

1½ cups smooth or chunky
    peanut butter and 2 cups
    Marshmallow Fluff® or
    Homemade Marshmallow
    Crème (see page 75) or
    Peanut Butter Filling (see
    page 76)

**Peanut butter and Marshmallow Fluff® is a classic combination in sandwiches and these whoopies are sure to appeal to peanut butter lovers everywhere.**

1 Preheat the oven to 375°F/190°C. Line 3–4 large baking sheets with parchment paper or grease the wells of a whoopie pan.

2 Put the butter, sugar, peanut butter, and vanilla extract in an electric mixer bowl, or use a large mixing bowl and a handheld electric mixer, and beat together until light and fluffy. Beat in the egg.

3 Sift the flour, baking soda, and salt into the bowl and stir together. Add the buttermilk and stir until combined.

4 Using a level 2-inch/5-cm ice-cream scoop or heaping tablespoon, make 24 halves. To make each half, put the batter onto the prepared sheets in 2-inch/5-cm-diameter rounds about 1¼ inches/3 cm high, or into the prepared pan. If you are using baking sheets, leave at least 3 inches/7.5 cm between each round to allow room for spreading.

5 Bake in the oven for 10–12 minutes, until firm to the touch. Transfer to a wire rack and let cool.

6 When the whoopies are cold, match each whoopie half with its closest partner in size. Spreading with a palette knife, cover the flat side of one whoopie half of each pair with peanut butter, then with Marshmallow Fluff® or Homemade Marshmallow Crème. Alternatively, spread generously with Peanut Butter Filling. Top each with its matching half, flat-side down, and press gently together.

## Plus One: Peanut Butter & Banana

Break a small banana into a large bowl, add ¼ teaspoon lemon juice, and mash with a fork. Sift in 6 cups confectioners' sugar. Add 4 tablespoons softened butter and beat together until smooth. Use to fill the whoopies in place of the filling options above.

# Summer

# Reverse Classic Whoopies

½ cup (1 stick) butter,
   softened, plus extra
   for greasing
1 cup granulated sugar
1 tsp vanilla extract
1 extra large egg
2⅓ cups all-purpose flour
1¼ tsp baking soda
pinch of salt
1 cup buttermilk
sifted confectioners' sugar,
   for dusting

*Filling*
Chocolate Buttercream
   (see page 73)

This recipe turns the traditional formula of Classic Whoopies (see page 20), namely chocolate sponge with a cream filling, on its head to offer two vanilla-flavored whoopies sandwiched together with a sumptuous chocolate filling.

1 Preheat the oven to 375°F/190°C. Line 3–4 large baking sheets with parchment paper or grease the wells of a whoopie pan.

2 Put the butter, sugar, and vanilla extract in an electric mixer bowl, or use a large mixing bowl and a handheld electric mixer, and beat together until light and fluffy. Beat in the egg.

3 Sift the flour, baking soda, and salt into the bowl and stir together. Add the buttermilk and stir until combined.

4 Using a level 2-inch/5-cm ice-cream scoop or heaping tablespoon, make 24 halves. To make each half, put the batter onto the prepared sheets in 2-inch/5-cm-diameter rounds about 1¼ inches/3 cm high, or into the prepared pan. If you are using baking sheets, leave at least 3 inches/7.5 cm between each round to allow room for spreading.

5 Bake in the oven for 10–12 minutes, until firm to the touch. Transfer to a wire rack and let cool.

6 When the whoopies are cold, match each whoopie half with its closest partner in size. Spreading with a palette knife or using a pastry bag fitted with a large star tip, cover the flat side of one whoopie half of each pair generously with the filling. Top each with its matching half, flat-side down, and press gently together.

7 Serve dusted with sifted confectioners' sugar.

## Plus One: Vanilla & Cardamom

Split a vanilla bean lengthwise with a sharp knife, scrape out the seeds, and add to the cake batter in place of the vanilla extract. Additionally, sift ¼ teaspoon ground cardamom in with the dry ingredients in Step 3, and, when making the buttercream, sift ½ teaspoon ground cardamom in with the confectioners' sugar and cocoa.

# Creamy Strawberry Whoopies

*Makes 10*

½ cup buttermilk
½ tsp vanilla extract
1½ tsp distilled white vinegar
½ cup (1 stick) butter,
    softened, plus extra
    for greasing
1 cup granulated sugar
1 extra large egg
2 cups all-purpose flour
½ tsp baking soda
pinch of salt
pink sugar flowers,
    for decorating

*Filling*

½ cup regular cream cheese
4 tbsp butter, softened
4¼ cups confectioners' sugar
¼ cup seedless strawberry
    conserve

*Topping*

1¾ cups confectioners' sugar
5–6 tsp hot water
red paste or liquid food
    coloring

**While no one could describe a whoopie as "dainty" as cakes go, these are undeniably and unashamedly pretty and "girlie."**

1 Preheat the oven to 375°F/190°C/170°C fan. Line 3–4 large baking sheets with parchment paper or grease the wells of a whoopie pan.

2 Put the buttermilk, vanilla extract, and vinegar in a pitcher and stir together.

3 Put the butter and sugar in an electric mixer bowl, or use a large mixing bowl and a handheld electric mixer, and beat together until light and fluffy. Beat in the egg.

4 Sift the flour, baking soda, and salt into the bowl and stir together. Add the buttermilk mixture and stir until combined.

5 Using a level 2-inch/5-cm ice-cream scoop or heaping tablespoon, make 20 halves. To make each half, put the batter onto the prepared sheets in 2-inch/5-cm-diameter rounds about 1¼ inches/3 cm high, or into the prepared pan. If you are using baking sheets, leave at least 3 inches/7.5 cm between each round to allow room for spreading.

6 Bake in the oven for 10–12 minutes, until firm to the touch. Transfer to a wire rack and let cool.

7 To make the filling, put the cream cheese and butter in a large bowl and beat together until smooth. Sift in the confectioners' sugar. Add the strawberry conserve and beat together until combined.

8 When the whoopies are cold, match each whoopie half with its closest partner in size. Spreading with a palette knife or using a pastry bag fitted with a large star tip, cover the flat side of one whoopie half of each pair generously with the filling. Top each with its matching half, flat-side down, and press gently together.

9 To make the topping, sift the confectioners' sugar into a bowl. Add the water and stir until the mixture is smooth and thick enough to coat the back of a wooden spoon. Dip the tip of a skewer into the food coloring, add to the icing, and stir until evenly colored. Spoon the icing on top of each filled whoopie. Decorate with sugar flowers and let set.

## Plus One: Creamy Raspberry

Use seedless raspberry jam instead of the strawberry conserve in the filling.

# Black Forest Whoopies

*Makes 12*

½ cup (1 stick) butter,
    softened, plus extra
    for greasing
1 cup granulated sugar
½ tsp vanilla extract
1 extra large egg
2 cups all-purpose flour
½ cup unsweetened cocoa
2½ tsp baking powder
pinch of salt
1 cup milk

*Filling*
15 oz/425 g canned pitted
    black cherries
2 tbsp Kirsch
1¼ cups heavy cream

Here, chocolate whoopies are luxuriously filled with black cherries and whipped cream, and moistened with a Kirsch-laced syrup to make mini versions of the beloved Black Forest Cake. These are ideal served as a dessert—strictly for grown-ups, of course.

1 Preheat the oven to 375°F/190°C. Line 3–4 large baking sheets with parchment paper or grease the wells of a whoopie pan.

2 Put the butter, sugar, and vanilla extract in an electric mixer bowl, or use a large mixing bowl and a handheld electric mixer, and beat together until light and fluffy. Beat in the egg.

3 Sift the flour, cocoa, baking powder, and salt into the bowl and stir together. Add the milk and stir until combined.

4 Using a level 2-inch/5-cm ice-cream scoop or heaping tablespoon, make 24 halves. To make each half, put the batter onto the prepared sheets in 2-inch/5-cm-diameter rounds about 1¼ inches/3 cm high, or into the prepared pan. If you are using baking sheets, leave at least 3 inches/7.5 cm between each round to allow room for spreading.

5 Bake in the oven for 10–12 minutes, until firm to the touch. Transfer to a wire rack and let cool.

6 To make the filling, drain the canned cherries, reserving the juice. Slice the cherries in half. Put 2 tablespoons of the reserved juice in a bowl and stir in the Kirsch. In a separate large bowl, whip the cream until stiff.

7 When the whoopies are cold, match each whoopie half with its closest partner in size. Spreading with a palette knife or using a pastry bag fitted with a large star tip, cover the flat side of the whoopie half of each pair generously with the whipped cream. Scatter the cherries on top. Top each with its matching half, flat-side down, and press gently together. Drizzle a teaspoon of the Kirsch syrup over the top of each whoopie.

## Plus One: Bursting Blueberry

Use 1½ cups fresh whole blueberries instead of the cherries and omit the Kirsch.
Fill the whoopies with the whipped cream as above and scatter over the blueberries.

# Apricot & Almond Whoopies

*Makes 12*

½ cup plumped dried
   apricots
4 tbsp butter, softened
½ cup ground almonds
1 cup granulated sugar
½ tsp almond extract
1 extra large egg
2⅓ cups all-purpose flour
1 tsp baking soda
pinch of salt
1 cup buttermilk

*Filling*
**Almond Buttercream**
   **(see page 73)**

**Two convenient pantry ingredients—dried apricots and ground almonds—are the feature flavorings in this whoopie recipe, and they were simply made for each other.**

1 Preheat the oven to 375°F/190°C. Line 3–4 large baking sheets with parchment paper or grease the wells of a whoopie pan.

2 Put the apricots in a food processor and pulse in short bursts until finely chopped.

3 Put the butter, ground almonds, sugar, and almond extract in an electric mixer bowl, or use a large mixing bowl and a handheld electric mixer, and beat together until light and fluffy. Beat in the egg.

4 Sift the flour, baking soda, and salt into the bowl and stir together. Add the buttermilk and chopped apricots and stir until combined.

5 Using a level 2-inch/5-cm ice-cream scoop or heaping tablespoon, make 24 halves. To make each half, put the batter onto the prepared sheets in 2-inch/5-cm-diameter rounds about 1¼ inches/3 cm high, or into the prepared pan. If you are using baking sheets, leave at least 3 inches/7.5 cm between each round to allow room for spreading.

6 Bake in the oven for 10–12 minutes, until firm to the touch. Transfer to a wire rack and let cool.

7 When the whoopies are cold, match each whoopie half with its closest partner in size. Spreading with a palette knife or using a pastry bag fitted with a large star tip, cover the flat side of one whoopie half of each pair generously with the filling. Top each with its matching half, flat-side down, and press gently together.

## Plus One: Cherry & Almond

Replace the apricots with the same quantity of candied cherries, chopping them by hand instead of in a food processor.

# Bashed Banana Whoopies

*Makes 10*

2 bananas

1 tsp lemon juice

½ cup (1 stick) butter, softened, plus extra for greasing

1 cup light brown sugar

1 tsp vanilla extract

1 extra large egg

2 cups all-purpose flour

½ tsp ground cinnamon

1 tsp baking powder

1 tsp baking soda

pinch of salt

3 tbsp sour cream

*Filling*

½ cup plus 1 tbsp (1⅛ sticks) butter, softened

3 cups confectioners' sugar

1 tbsp milk

1 tbsp honey

**Packed with good-for-you bananas, perhaps these moist whoopies could almost be classed as health food! Whatever else, they are sure to enhance well-being by lifting the spirits.**

1 Preheat the oven to 375°F/190°C. Line 3–4 large baking sheets with parchment paper or grease the wells of a whoopie pan.

2 Break the bananas into a bowl. Add the lemon juice and mash together with a fork until smooth.

3 Put the butter, sugar, and vanilla extract in an electric mixer bowl, or use a large mixing bowl and a handheld electric mixer, and beat together until light and fluffy. Beat in the egg.

4 Sift the flour, cinnamon, baking powder, baking soda, and salt into the bowl and stir together. Add the mashed bananas and sour cream and stir until combined.

5 Using a level 2-inch/5-cm ice-cream scoop or heaping tablespoon, make 20 halves. To make each half, put the batter onto the prepared sheets in 2-inch/5-cm-diameter rounds about 1¼ inches/3 cm high, or into the prepared pan. If you are using baking sheets, leave at least 3 inches/7.5 cm between each round to allow room for spreading.

6 Bake in the oven for 10 minutes, until firm to the touch. Transfer to a wire rack and let cool.

7 To make the filling, put the butter in a large bowl. Sift in the confectioners' sugar. Add the milk and honey and beat together until smooth.

8 When the whoopies are cold, match each whoopie half with its closest partner in size. Spreading with a palette knife or using a pastry bag fitted with a large star tip, cover the flat side of one whoopie half of each pair generously with the filling. Top each with its matching half, flat-side down, and press gently together.

## Plus One: Banana & Passion Fruit

Cut 4 passion fruits in half, scoop out the pulp, and put in a small saucepan. Add 4 tablespoons honey and heat gently until warmed through. Spoon the mixture over the filled whoopies.

Fall

# Pumpkin Whoopies

½ cup (1 stick) butter,
    softened, plus extra
    for greasing
1 cup light brown sugar
1 tsp vanilla extract
1 extra large egg
2⅓ cups all-purpose flour
1 tsp baking powder
1 tsp baking soda
1 tsp ground cinnamon
½ tsp ground ginger
¼ tsp ground allspice or
    grated nutmeg
¼ tsp ground cloves
pinch of salt
1 cup canned or fresh
    pumpkin purée
2 tbsp buttermilk

*Filling*
Cream Cheese Filling
    (see page 76)

Although sure to be popular all the year round, these sweet-spicy pumpkin-packed whoopies are particularly good for Halloween or Thanksgiving. You could even serve them as a contemporary take on the traditional pumpkin pie.

1 Preheat the oven to 375°F/190°C. Line 3–4 large baking sheets with parchment paper or grease the wells of a whoopie pan.

2 Put the butter, sugar, and vanilla extract in an electric mixer bowl, or use a large mixing bowl and a handheld electric mixer, and beat together until light and fluffy. Beat in the egg.

3 Sift the flour, baking powder, baking soda, cinnamon, ginger, allspice, cloves, and salt into the bowl and stir together. Add the pumpkin and buttermilk and stir until combined.

4 Using a level 2-inch/5-cm ice-cream scoop or heaping tablespoon, make 24 halves. To make each half, put the batter onto the prepared sheets in 2-inch/5-cm-diameter rounds about 1¼ inches/3 cm high, or into the prepared pan. If you are using baking sheets, leave at least 3 inches/7.5 cm between each round to allow room for spreading.

5 Bake in the oven for 10–12 minutes, until firm to the touch. Transfer to a wire rack and let cool.

6 When the whoopies are cold, match each whoopie half with its closest partner in size. Spreading with a palette knife or using a pastry bag fitted with a large star tip, cover the flat side of one whoopie half of each pair generously with the filling. Top each with its matching half, flat-side down, and press gently together.

## Plus One: Pumpkin & Banana

Slice 2 bananas, put in a bowl, and toss with ½ teaspoon lemon juice. Spread half the generous quantity of Cream Cheese Filling called for above on one half of each pair of whoopies, arrange the sliced bananas on top, and cover each with its matching half.

# Chocolate Chunk & Oat Whoopies

½ cup (1 stick) butter,
    softened, plus extra
    for greasing
1 cup light brown sugar
½ tsp vanilla extract
1 extra large egg
2⅓ cups all-purpose flour
2½ tsp baking powder
pinch of salt
heaping ½ cup semisweet
    chocolate chunks
⅔ cup rolled oats
¼ tbsp buttermilk

*Filling*
**Vanilla Buttercream
    (see page 73)**

**Semisweet chocolate chunks are always irresistible, and combined with oats for extra crunch, these whoopies are especially satisfying— it will be difficult to eat just one.**

1 Preheat the oven to 375°F/190°C. Line 3–4 large baking sheets with parchment paper or butter the wells of a whoopie pan.

2 Put the butter, sugar, and vanilla extract in an electric mixer bowl, or use a large mixing bowl and a handheld electric mixer, and beat together until light and fluffy. Beat in the egg.

3 Sift the flour, baking powder, and salt into the bowl and stir together. Add the chocolate chunks, oats, and buttermilk and stir until combined.

4 Using a level 2-inch/5-cm ice-cream scoop or heaping tablespoon, make 24 halves. To make each half, put the batter onto the prepared sheets in 2-inch/5-cm-diameter rounds about 1¼ inches/3 cm high, or into the prepared pan. If you are using baking sheets, leave at least 3 inches/7.5 cm between each round to allow room for spreading.

5 Bake in the oven for 10–12 minutes, until firm to the touch. Transfer to a wire rack and let cool.

6 When the whoopies are cold, match each whoopie half with its closest partner in size. Spreading with a palette knife or using a pastry bag fitted with a large star tip, cover the flat side of one whoopie half of each pair generously with the filling. Top each with its matching half, flat-side down, and press gently together.

## Plus One: Soft Fudge

In place of the chocolate chunks, add the same quantity of fudge pieces to the whoopie cake batter, and replace the filling with Butterscotch Filling (see page 78).

# Moist Apple & Almond Whoopies

*Makes 10*

2 apples
½ tsp lemon juice
½ cup (1 stick) butter,
    softened, plus extra
    for greasing
1 cup granulated sugar
½ tsp almond extract
1 extra large egg
2⅓ cups all-purpose flour
2½ tsp baking powder
pinch of salt
2 tbsp slivered almonds

*Filling*
Vanilla Buttercream
    (see page 73)

This is another winning fruit 'n' nut combination. Grated apples bring a pleasing moistness to the whoopies, while almond extract enhances their flavor without the addition of relatively expensive ground almonds—although you would never guess.

1 Preheat the oven to 375°F/190°C. Line 3–4 large baking sheets with parchment paper or grease the wells of a whoopie pan.

2 Peel, core, and grate the apples. Put in a bowl, add the lemon juice, and toss together.

3 Put the butter, sugar, and almond extract in an electric mixer bowl, or use a large mixing bowl and a handheld electric mixer, and beat together until light and fluffy. Beat in the egg.

4 Sift the flour, baking powder, and salt into the bowl and stir together. Add the grated apple and stir until combined.

5 Using a level 2-inch/5-cm ice-cream scoop or heaping tablespoon, make 20 halves. To make each half, put the batter onto the prepared sheets in 2-inch/5-cm-diameter rounds about 1¼ inches/3 cm high, or into the prepared pan. If you are using baking sheets, leave at least 3 inches/7.5 cm between each round to allow room for spreading.

6 Sprinkle the slivered almonds equally on top of 10 of the mounds of batter.

7 Bake in the oven for 10–12 minutes, until firm to the touch. Transfer to a wire rack and let cool.

8 When the whoopies are cold, match each almond-topped whoopie half with its closest partner in size. Spreading with a palette knife or using a pastry bag fitted with a large star tip, cover the flat side of each whoopie half without almonds generously with the filling. Top each with its matching almond-topped half, flat-side down, and press gently together.

## Plus One: Toffee Apple

Omit the almond extract and slivered almonds. Fill the whoopies with Caramel Buttercream (see page 73) and drizzle about 1 teaspoon dulce de leche over the top of each.

# Green Pistachio Whoopies

*Makes 10*

heaping ⅓ cup shelled
  pistachios
½ cup buttermilk
½ tsp vanilla extract
½ tsp green paste food
  coloring
1½ tsp distilled white vinegar
½ cup (1 stick) butter,
  softened, plus extra
  for greasing
1 cup granulated sugar
1 extra large egg
2 cups all-purpose flour
½ tsp baking soda
pinch of salt

*Filling*
**Homemade Marshmallow
  Crème (see page 75)
  or Classic Marshmallow
  Filling (see page 73)**

There's no other way to describe these—whoopies tinted an attractive shade of green to reflect the distinctive color of the finely chopped pistachios that flavor them.

1 Preheat the oven to 375°F/190°C. Line 3–4 large baking sheets with parchment paper or grease the wells of a whoopie pan.

2 Finely chop the pistachios.

3 Put the buttermilk, vanilla extract, green food coloring, and vinegar in a bowl and stir together.

4 Put the butter and sugar in an electric mixer bowl, or use a large mixing bowl and a handheld electric mixer, and beat together until light and fluffy. Beat in the egg.

5 Sift the flour, baking soda, and salt into the bowl and stir together. Add the chopped pistachios, reserving 1 tablespoon, and the buttermilk mixture and beat until well combined.

6 Using a level 2-inch/5-cm ice-cream scoop or heaping tablespoon, make 20 halves. To make each half, put the batter onto the prepared sheets in 2-inch/5-cm-diameter rounds about 1¼ inches/3 cm high, or into the prepared pan. If you are using baking sheets, leave at least 3 inches/7.5 cm between each round to allow room for spreading. Sprinkle the reserved pistachios equally on top of 10 of the mounds of batter.

7 Bake in the oven for 10–12 minutes, until firm to the touch. Transfer to a wire rack and let cool.

8 When the whoopies are cold, match each pistachio-topped whoopie half with its closest partner in size. Spreading with a palette knife or using a pastry bag fitted with a large star tip, cover the flat side of each whoopie half without pistachios generously with the filling. Top each with its matching pistachio-topped half, flat-side down, and press gently together.

## Plus One: Crunchy Hazelnut

Omit the food coloring and replace the pistachios with hazelnuts, both in the batter and for sprinkling. Instead of the filling, spread the whoopie halves without hazelnuts generously with store-bought hazelnut-and-chocolate spread, then sprinkle with ¾ cup chopped hazelnuts before covering with the matching hazelnut-topped halves.

# Mocha Whoopies

*Makes 9*

3 tbsp instant espresso
   coffee powder
1 tbsp boiling water
½ cup (1 stick) butter,
   softened, plus extra
   for greasing
1 cup dark brown sugar
1 extra large egg
2 cups all-purpose flour
½ cup unsweetened cocoa
1¼ tsp baking soda
pinch of salt
2 tbsp buttermilk

*Filling*
Chocolate Marshmallow
   Crème (see page 75)

**Dark, rich, and seductive, these mini mochas are guaranteed to appeal to coffee and chocolate addicts alike.**

1 Preheat the oven to 375°F/190°C. Line 3–4 large baking sheets with parchment paper or grease the wells of a whoopie pan.

2 Dissolve the coffee in the boiling water and set aside to cool.

3 Put the butter and sugar in an electric mixer bowl, or use a large mixing bowl and a handheld electric mixer, and beat together until light and fluffy. Beat in the egg.

4 Sift the flour, cocoa, baking soda, and salt into the bowl and stir together. Add the coffee and buttermilk and stir until combined.

5 Using a level 2-inch/5-cm ice-cream scoop or heaping tablespoon, make 18 halves. To make each half, put the batter onto the prepared sheets in 2-inch/5-cm-diameter rounds about 1¼ inches/3 cm high, or into the prepared pan. If you are using baking sheets, leave at least 3 inches/7.5 cm between each round to allow room for spreading.

6 Bake in the oven for 10–12 minutes, until firm to the touch. Transfer to a wire rack and let cool.

7 When the whoopies are cold, match each whoopie half with its closest partner in size. Spreading with a palette knife or using a pastry bag fitted with a large star tip, cover the flat side of one whoopie half of each pair generously with the filling. Top each with its matching half, flat-side down, and press gently together.

## Plus One: Tiramisù

In place of the Chocolate Marshmallow Crème filling, put ½ cup mascarpone cheese and 5 tablespoons softened butter in a large bowl and beat together. Sift in 4½ cups confectioners' sugar and beat until combined. Use to fill the whoopies. Drizzle about 1 teaspoon Marsala over the top of each to finish.

# Winter

# Mint Chocolate Whoopies

*Makes 12*

½ cup (1 stick) butter,
　softened, plus extra
　for greasing
1 cup granulated sugar
1 tsp vanilla extract
1 extra large egg
2 cups all-purpose flour
½ cup unsweetened cocoa
2½ tsp baking powder
pinch of salt
1 cup milk
heaping ½ cup semisweet
　chocolate chips

*Filling*

¾ cup (1½ sticks) butter,
　softened
½ tsp mint extract
3½ cups confectioners' sugar
1 tbsp milk or cream
green paste or liquid food
　coloring

**It's all in the filling—a cool green minty buttercream, contrasted against the warm brown of chocolate whoopies studded with chocolate chips. In short, the perfect partnership.**

1 Preheat the oven to 375°F/190°C. Line 3–4 large baking sheets with parchment paper or grease the wells of a whoopie pan.

2 Put the butter, sugar, and vanilla extract in an electric mixer bowl, or use a large mixing bowl and a handheld electric mixer, and beat together until light and fluffy. Beat in the egg.

3 Sift the flour, cocoa, baking powder, and salt into the bowl and stir together. Add the milk and chocolate chips and stir until combined.

4 Using a level 2-inch/5-cm ice-cream scoop or heaping tablespoon, make 24 halves. To make each half, put the batter onto the prepared sheets in 2-inch/5-cm-diameter rounds about 1¼ inches/3 cm high, or into the prepared pan. If you are using baking sheets, leave at least 3 inches/7.5 cm between each round to allow room for spreading.

5 Bake in the oven for 10–12 minutes, until firm to the touch. Transfer to a wire rack and let cool.

6 For the filling, put the butter and mint extract in a large bowl and beat together with a wooden spoon until light and fluffy. Sift in the confectioners' sugar. Add the milk and beat together until well blended. Dip the tip of a skewer into the food coloring, add to the filling, and stir until evenly colored to the shade that you want.

7 When the whoopies are cold, match each whoopie half with its closest partner in size. Spreading with a palette knife or using a pastry bag fitted with a large star tip, cover the flat side of one whoopie half of each pair generously with the filling. Top each with its matching half, flat-side down, and press gently together.

## Plus One: Chocolate & Ginger

Replace the mint filling with Ginger Buttercream (see page 73).

# Gingerbread Whoopies

Makes 9

½ cup plus 3 tbsp (1⅜ sticks)
   butter, softened, plus extra
   for greasing
¾ cup dark brown sugar
1 tsp vanilla extract
1 extra large egg
2 tbsp molasses or
   blackstrap molasses
2⅓ cups all-purpose flour
2½ tsp baking powder
1½ tsp ground ginger
¾ tsp ground allspice
pinch of salt
1 tbsp milk

*Filling*
Lemon Buttercream
   (see page 73)

**This classic recipe is beloved by both children and adults. The whoopies are filled with a zesty lemon-flavored buttercream, which provides the ideal foil for the warm, mellow spices.**

1 Preheat the oven to 375°F/190°C. Line 3–4 large baking sheets with parchment paper or grease the wells of a whoopie pan.

2 Put the butter, sugar, and vanilla extract in an electric mixer bowl, or use a large mixing bowl and a handheld electric mixer, and beat together until light and fluffy. Add the egg and molasses and beat together.

3 Sift the flour, baking powder, ginger, allspice, and salt into the bowl and stir together. Add the milk and stir until combined.

4 Using a level 2-inch/5-cm ice-cream scoop or heaping tablespoon, make 18 halves. To make each half, put the batter onto the prepared sheets in 2-inch/5-cm-diameter rounds about 1¼ inches/3 cm high, or into the prepared pan. If you are using baking sheets, leave at least 3 inches/7.5 cm between each round to allow room for spreading.

5 Bake in the oven for 10–12 minutes, until firm to the touch. Transfer to a wire rack and let cool.

6 When the whoopies are cold, match each whoopie half with its closest partner in size. Spreading with a palette knife or using a pastry bag fitted with a large star tip, cover the flat side of one whoopie half of each pair generously with the filling. Top each with its matching half, flat-side down, and press gently together.

## Plus One: Brown Sugar & Spice

For the whoopie batter, omit the ground ginger and increase the allspice to 2 teaspoons. Instead of the buttercream, fill the whoopies with Butterscotch Filling (see page 78).

# Citrus Orange Whoopies

½ cup plus 3 tbsp (1⅜ sticks)
   butter, softened, plus extra
   for greasing
¾ cup granulated sugar
1 extra large egg
2⅓ cups all-purpose flour
2½ tsp baking powder
pinch of salt
finely grated rind of
   2 oranges
3 tbsp orange juice
shredded orange rind,
   for decorating

*Filling*
Orange Buttercream
   (see page 73)

*Topping*
1¾ cups confectioners' sugar
5–6 tsp orange juice
orange paste or liquid
   food coloring

These extra-soft whoopies offer bold orange flavor throughout—in the cake, filling, topping and even the final decorative touch. Fresh strawberries make a nice accompaniment.

1 Preheat the oven to 375°F/190°C. Line 3–4 large baking sheets with parchment paper or grease the wells of a whoopie pan.

2 Put the butter and sugar in an electric mixer bowl, or use a large mixing bowl and a handheld electric mixer, and beat together until light and fluffy. Beat in the egg.

3 Sift the flour, baking powder, and salt into the bowl and stir together. Add the grated orange rind and juice and stir until combined.

4 Using a level 2-inch/5-cm ice-cream scoop or heaping tablespoon, make 20 halves. To make each half, put the batter onto the prepared sheets in 2-inch/5-cm-diameter rounds about 1¼ inches/3 cm high, or into the prepared pan. If you are using baking sheets, leave at least 3 inches/7.5 cm between each round to allow room for spreading.

5 Bake in the oven for 10–12 minutes, until firm to the touch. Transfer to a wire rack and let cool.

6 When the whoopies are cold, match each whoopie half with its closest partner in size. Spreading with a palette knife or using a pastry bag fitted with a large star tip, cover the flat side of one whoopie half of each pair generously with the filling. Top each with its matching half, flat-side down, and press gently together.

7 For the topping, sift the confectioners' sugar into a bowl. Add the orange juice and stir until the mixture is smooth and thick enough to coat the back of a wooden spoon. Dip the tip of a skewer into the food coloring, add to the icing and stir until evenly colored to the shade that you want.

8 Spoon the topping over each whoopie. Top with shredded orange rind to decorate and let set.

## Plus One: Lemon & Poppy Seed

Replace the grated orange rind and juice with grated lemon rind and juice and add to the whoopie batter along with 2 tablespoons poppy seeds. Instead of the buttercream, fill the whoopies with Cream Cheese Filling (see page 76) and decorate with shredded lemon rind.

# Very Chocolate Whoopies

Whoopie purists fervently believe that the whoopie should be chocolate and nothing else, while others view whoopies as the next best thing to Oreo cookies. Combine the two and you get the very best chocolate whoopies ever. These are definitely ones for sharing.

*Makes 12*

3½ oz/100 g semisweet
  chocolate (minimum
  70% cocoa solids)
½ cup (1 stick) butter,
  softened, plus extra
  for greasing
1 cup granulated sugar
1 tsp vanilla extract
1 large egg
2 cups all-purpose flour
½ cup unsweetened cocoa
2½ tsp baking powder
pinch of salt
1 cup milk
12 mini Oreo cookies,
  for decorating

*Filling*
Oreo Cream Filling
  (see page 78)

*Topping*
Chocolate Ganache
  (see page 81)

1 Preheat the oven to 375°F/190°C/170°C fan. Line 3–4 large baking sheets with parchment paper or grease the wells of a whoopie pan.

2 Finely grate the chocolate or put in a food processor and process until very finely ground. Set aside.

3 Put the butter, sugar, and vanilla extract in an electric mixer bowl, or use a large mixing bowl and a handheld electric mixer, and beat together until light and fluffy. Beat in the egg.

4 Sift the flour, cocoa, baking powder, and salt into the bowl and stir together. Add the chocolate and milk and stir until combined.

5 Using a level 2-inch/5-cm ice-cream scoop or heaping tablespoon, make 24 halves. To make each half, put the batter onto the prepared sheets in 2-inch/5-cm-diameter rounds about 1¼ inches/3 cm high, or into the prepared pan. If you are using baking sheets, leave at least 3 inches/7.5 cm between each round to allow room for spreading.

6 Bake in the oven for 10–12 minutes, until firm to the touch. Transfer to a wire rack and let cool.

7 When the whoopies are cold, match each whoopie half with its closest partner in size. Spreading with a palette knife or using a pastry bag fitted with a large star tip, cover the flat side of one whoopie half of each pair generously with the filling.

8 Spread the Chocolate Ganache on top of the other whoopie halves, then place each on top of its matching bottom half and press gently together. Decorate each with a mini Oreo cookie and let set.

## Plus One: Chocolate & Butterscotch

Instead of the Oreo Cream Filling, use the Butterscotch Filling (see page 78) to fill the whoopies, omit the ganache topping, and dust with sifted confectioners' sugar before serving.

# Pecan & Maple Syrup Whoopies

*Makes 12*

heaping ½ cup pecan halves
½ cup plus 3 tbsp (1⅜ sticks)
    butter, softened, plus extra
    for greasing
¾ cup light brown sugar
1 tsp vanilla extract
1 extra large egg
2⅓ cups all-purpose flour
2½ tsp baking powder
pinch of salt
scant ⅔ cup maple syrup
¼ cup milk

*Filling*
**Butterscotch Filling
    (see page 78)**

**These whoopies are wonderfully moist and syrupy, and the addition of chopped pecans gives them a little winter flair.**

1 Preheat the oven to 375°F/190°C. Line 3–4 large baking sheets with parchment paper or butter the wells of a whoopie pan.

2 Reserve 12 of the smallest pecan halves. Finely chop the remaining pecan halves and set aside.

3 Put the butter, sugar, and vanilla extract in an electric mixer bowl, or use a large mixing bowl and a handheld electric mixer, and beat together until light and fluffy. Beat in the egg.

4 Sift the flour, baking powder, and salt into the bowl and stir together. Add the chopped pecans, maple syrup, and milk and stir until combined.

5 Using a level 2-inch/5-cm ice-cream scoop or heaping tablespoon, make 24 halves. To make each half, put the batter onto the prepared sheets in 2-inch/5-cm-diameter rounds about 1¼ inches/3 cm high, or into the prepared pan. If you are using baking sheets, leave at least 3 inches/7.5 cm between each round to allow room for spreading. Put one of the reserved pecan halves on top of each of 12 mounds of batter.

6 Bake in the oven for 10–12 minutes, until firm to the touch. Transfer to a wire rack and let cool.

7 When the whoopies are cold, match each pecan-topped whoopie half with its closest partner in size. Spreading with a palette knife or using a pastry bag fitted with a large star tip, cover the flat side of each whoopie half without a pecan generously with the filling. Top each with its matching half, flat-side down, and press gently together.

## Plus One: Winter Walnut

Simply replace the pecans with walnuts and use honey instead of the maple syrup.

# Making Whoopies

# Mix & Match

Having mastered the main whoopie recipes, this is the opportunity to get creative. The basic Chocolate Whoopies and the basic Vanilla Whoopies are the recipes that you will keep returning to. These are given here, along with a collection of all the fillings and toppings that you will ever need for easy reference. The possibilities are endless.

## Vanilla Whoopies

*Makes 12*

½ cup (1 stick) butter, softened, plus extra for greasing
1 cup granulated sugar
1 tsp vanilla extract
1 extra large egg
2⅓ cups all-purpose flour
1¼ tsp baking soda
pinch of salt
1 cup buttermilk

1  Preheat the oven to 375°F/190°C. Line 3–4 large baking sheets with parchment paper or grease the wells of a whoopie pan.

2  Put the butter, sugar, and vanilla extract in an electric mixer bowl, or use a large mixing bowl and a handheld electric mixer, and beat together until light and fluffy. Beat in the egg.

3  Sift the flour, baking soda, and salt into the bowl and stir together. Add the buttermilk and stir until combined.

4  Using a level 2-inch/5-cm ice-cream scoop or heaping tablespoon, make 24 halves. To make each half, put the batter onto the prepared sheets in 2-inch/5-cm-diameter rounds about 1¼ inches/3 cm high, or into the prepared pan. If you are using baking sheets, leave at least 3 inches/7.5 cm between each round to allow room for spreading.

5  Bake in the oven for 10–12 minutes, until firm to the touch. Transfer to a wire rack and let cool.

6  When the whoopies are cold, match each whoopie half with its closest partner in size and then fill and decorate as desired.

# Chocolate Whoopies

*Makes 12*

½ cup (1 stick) butter, softened, plus extra for greasing
1 cup dark brown sugar
1 tsp vanilla extract
1 extra large egg
2 cups all-purpose flour
½ cup unsweetened cocoa
1¼ tsp baking soda
pinch of salt
1 cup buttermilk

1 Preheat the oven to 375°F/190°C. Line 3–4 large baking sheets with parchment paper or grease the wells of a whoopie pan.

2 Put the butter, sugar, and vanilla extract in an electric mixer bowl, or use a large mixing bowl and a handheld electric mixer, and beat together until light and fluffy. Beat in the egg.

3 Sift the flour, cocoa, baking soda, and salt into the bowl and stir together. Add the buttermilk and stir until combined.

4 Using a level 2-inch/5-cm ice-cream scoop or heaping tablespoon, make 24 halves. To make each half, put the batter onto the prepared sheets in 2-inch/5-cm-diameter rounds about 1¼ inches/3 cm high, or into the prepared pan. If you are using baking sheets, leave at least 3 inches/7.5 cm between each round to allow room for spreading.

5 Bake in the oven for 10–12 minutes, until firm to the touch. Transfer to a wire rack and let cool.

6 When the whoopies are cold, match each whoopie half with its closest partner in size and then fill and decorate as desired.

# Mini Chocolate Whoopies

*Makes 24*

½ cup (1 stick) butter, softened, plus extra for greasing
1 cup granulated sugar
½ tsp vanilla extract
1 extra large egg
2 cups all-purpose flour
½ cup unsweetened cocoa
2½ tsp baking powder
pinch of salt
1 cup milk

1 Preheat the oven to 375°F/190°C. Line 3–4 large baking sheets with parchment paper or grease the cups of a 24-cup mini muffin pan.

2 Put the butter, sugar, and vanilla extract in an electric mixer bowl, or use a large mixing bowl and a handheld electric mixer, and beat together until light and fluffy. Beat in the egg.

3 Sift the flour, cocoa, baking powder, and salt into the bowl and stir together. Add the milk and stir until combined.

4 Using a heaping teaspoon, put the batter onto the prepared baking sheets, allowing room for spreading, or in the prepared pan.

5 Bake in the oven for 8–10 minutes, until firm to the touch. Transfer to a wire rack and let cool.

6 When cold, fill and decorate as desired.

# Mini Vanilla Whoopies

*Makes 24*

½ cup (1 stick) butter, softened, plus extra for greasing
1 cup granulated sugar
½ tsp vanilla extract
1 extra large egg
2¼ cups all-purpose flour
2½ tsp baking powder
pinch of salt
1 cup milk

1 Preheat the oven to 375°F/190°C. Line 3–4 large baking sheets with parchment paper or grease the cups of a 24-cup mini muffin pan.

2 Put the butter, sugar, and vanilla extract in an electric mixer bowl, or use a large mixing bowl and a handheld electric mixer, and beat together until light and fluffy. Beat in the egg.

3 Sift the flour, baking powder, and salt into the bowl and stir together. Add the milk and stir until combined.

4 Using a heaping teaspoon, put the batter onto the prepared baking sheets, allowing room for spreading, or in the prepared pan.

5 Bake in the oven for 8–10 minutes, until firm to the touch. Transfer to a wire rack and let cool.

6 When cold, fill and decorate as desired.

# Vanilla Buttercream

*Makes enough to fill 12 whoopies*
¾ cup (1½ sticks) butter, softened
¾ tsp vanilla extract
3½ cups confectioners' sugar
1 tbsp milk or cream

1 Put the butter and vanilla extract in a large bowl and beat together with a wooden spoon until combined.

2 Sift in the confectioners' sugar. Add the milk and beat together until light and fluffy. Use immediately or store in the refrigerator for up to 1 week.

VARIATIONS
### Chocolate Buttercream
Replace ½ cup of the confectioners' sugar with the same quantity of unsweetened cocoa.

### Almond Buttercream
Replace the vanilla extract with ³/₄ teaspoon almond extract.

### Coffee Buttercream
Dissolve 1 tablespoon instant espresso powder in 1 teaspoon boiling water. Let stand until cold and use instead of the vanilla extract.

### Caramel Buttercream
Add 2 tablespoons of dulce de leche with the milk.

### Ginger Buttercream
Use the syrup from a jar of preserved ginger in syrup instead of the milk or cream and add 4 pieces of finely chopped preserved ginger to the buttercream.

### Colored Buttercream
Using paste or liquid food coloring of your choice, such as red, green, or yellow, dip the tip of a skewer into the coloring, add to the buttercream, and stir until evenly colored to the shade desired.

### Orange or Lemon Buttercream
Replace the milk or cream with orange or lemon juice. Add a little finely grated rind, and color with orange or yellow food coloring, as in Colored Buttercream, if desired.

# Classic Marshmallow Filling

*Makes enough to fill 12 whoopies*
1 cup confectioners' sugar
½ cup (1 stick) butter or vegetable shortening, softened
⅔ cup Marshmallow Fluff®
1 tsp vanilla extract

1 Sift the confectioners' sugar into a bowl.

2 Put the butter and Marshmallow Fluff® in an electric mixer bowl, or use a large mixing bowl and a handheld electric mixer, and beat together for about 3 minutes until light and fluffy.

3 On a low speed, gradually add the confectioners' sugar in spoonfuls. Add the vanilla extract and beat together for about an additional 3 minutes, until combined.

4 Use immediately or store in the refrigerator for up to 2–3 days.

## Homemade Marshmallow Crème

*Makes enough to fill 12 whoopies*

heaping ½ cup confectioners' sugar
1 extra large egg white
½ cup light corn syrup
pinch of salt

1 Sift the confectioners' sugar into a bowl.

2 Put the egg white, syrup, and salt in an electric mixer bowl, or use a large mixing bowl and a handheld electric mixer, and beat on high speed for 5 minutes, until thick and doubled in volume.

3 On low speed, gradually add the confectioners' sugar in spoonfuls. Beat until combined.

4 Use immediately or store in the refrigerator for up to 2–3 days. The filling is suitable for spreading instead of piping into whoopies.

## Chocolate Marshmallow Crème

*Makes enough to fill 12 whoopies*

1¾ oz/50 g semisweet chocolate
1¾ cups confectioners' sugar
1 extra large egg white
⅓ cup light corn syrup
pinch of salt

1 Break the chocolate into a heatproof bowl. Melt in a microwave oven on High for 30 seconds. Stir with a tablespoon. Cook again on High, checking and stirring every 10 seconds, until smooth. Alternatively, put the bowl over a saucepan of simmering water, making sure the bottom of the bowl doesn't touch the water, and stir until smooth. Let stand until cold but not set.

2 Sift the confectioners' sugar into a bowl.

3 Put the egg white, syrup, and salt in an electric mixer bowl, or use a large mixing bowl and a handheld electric mixer, and beat on high speed for 5 minutes, until thick and doubled in volume.

4 On low speed, gradually add the confectioners' sugar in spoonfuls. Add the melted chocolate and beat until just combined.

5 Chill in the refrigerator for 3–4 hours before using, and store for up to 2–3 days. The filling is suitable for spreading instead of piping into whoopies.

## Peanut Butter Filling

*Makes enough to fill 12 whoopies*
1 cup plus 3 tbsp smooth or chunky peanut butter
½ cup plus 2 tbsp (1¼ sticks) butter, softened
heaping 1 cup confectioners' sugar

1 Put the peanut butter and butter in a large bowl and
  beat together with a wooden spoon until smooth.

2 Sift in the confectioners' sugar and beat together
  until light and fluffy. Use immediately or store in the
  refrigerator for up to 2–3 days.

## Cream Cheese Filling

*Makes enough to fill 12 whoopies*
½ cup regular cream cheese
5 tbsp butter, softened
½ tsp vanilla extract
4½ cups confectioners' sugar

1 Put the cream cheese, butter, and vanilla extract in
  a large bowl and beat together with a wooden spoon
  until light and fluffy.

2 Sift in the confectioners' sugar and beat together
  until well combined. Use immediately or store in
  the refrigerator for up to 2–3 days.

## Butterscotch Filling

*Makes enough to fill 12 whoopies*
4 tbsp butter
½ cup light brown sugar
⅓ cup evaporated milk
4 cups confectioners' sugar
½ tsp vanilla extract

1 Put the butter, sugar, and evaporated milk in a saucepan. Heat gently, stirring all the time, until the butter has melted. Remove from the heat and let cool slightly.

2 Sift in the confectioners' sugar. Add the vanilla extract and beat well until combined. Let cool before using. Store in the refrigerator for up to 1 week.

## Oreo Cream Filling

*Makes enough to fill 12 whoopies*
3 Oreo cookies
4 tbsp butter, softened
½ cup regular cream cheese
3½ cups confectioners' sugar

1 Put the cookies in a strong plastic bag and, holding the open end together, crush with a rolling pin to form fine crumbs.

2 Put the butter and cream cheese in an electric mixer bowl, or use a large mixing bowl and a hand-held electric mixer, and beat together until light and fluffy.

3 Sift in the confectioners' sugar and beat together until smooth but still firm.

4 Using a tablespoon, fold in the cookie crumbs. Use immediately or store in the refrigerator for up to 2–3 days.

# Sugar Glaze

*Makes enough to cover 12 whoopies*
1¾ cups confectioners' sugar
5–6 tsp hot water

1 Sift the confectioners' sugar into a bowl. Add the hot water and stir until the mixture is smooth and thick enough to coat the back of a wooden spoon. Use immediately and let set.

VARIATIONS
### Chocolate Glaze
Replace 3 tablespoons of the confectioners' sugar with 3 tablespoons unsweetened cocoa.

### Coffee Glaze
Dissolve 1 tablespoon instant coffee granules in 1 tablespoon boiling water. Let cool and then mix with the confectioners' sugar in place of the water, adding a little extra water, if necessary.

### Mocha Glaze
Replace 3 tablespoons of the confectioners' sugar with 3 tablespoons unsweetened cocoa. Dissolve 2 teaspoons instant coffee granules in 1 tablespoon boiling water. Let cool and then mix with the confectioners' sugar in place of the water, adding a little extra water, if necessary.

### Colored Glaze
Using paste or liquid food coloring of your choice, such as red, green, or yellow, dip the tip of a skewer into the coloring, add to the frosting, and stir until evenly colored to the shade desired.

### Orange or Lemon Glaze
Replace the water with orange or lemon juice, and color with orange or yellow food coloring, as in Colored Glaze, if desired.

# Chocolate Ganache

*Makes enough to cover 12 whoopies*
5½ oz/150 g semisweet chocolate
⅔ cup heavy cream
small pat of butter

1 Break the chocolate into a heatproof bowl and add the cream. Put the bowl over a saucepan of simmering water and heat until the chocolate has melted, stirring constantly.

2 Remove from the heat and add the butter. Stir until smooth and shiny. Let cool for about 2 hours, stirring occasionally, until firm enough to spread. Store in the refrigerator for up to 2–3 days and return to room temperature before using.

# Party Decorating Ideas

## Children's Birthday Whoopies

Bake a batch of Chocolate or Vanilla Whoopies. Fill with Chocolate Buttercream. Cover with Chocolate or Colored Glaze and let set. Dust with cake sprinkles and add a candle to each.

## Children's Party Box

Bake a batch of Chocolate Whoopies. Fill with Chocolate Buttercream. Cover with Chocolate Glaze. Sprinkle with candy-coated chocolate candies and let set. Pack individually in a box to take home.

## After-Dinner Whoopies

Bake a batch of Mini Chocolate Whoopies. Spread the bottom halves with Chocolate Buttercream. Cover the top halves with Chocolate Ganache, put on top of the bottom halves, and let set. Put the filled whoopies in a small dish to serve.

## Host & Hostess Whoopies

Bake a batch of Mini Vanilla Whoopies. Spread the bottom halves with Chocolate Buttercream or Chocolate Marshmallow Crème. Cover the top halves with Chocolate Ganache, put on top of the bottom halves, and let set. Pack in a box to give as a gift.

## Valentine Whoopies

Make for an engagement party or any other romantic celebration. Bake a batch of Red Velvet Whoopies (see page 22). Using a heart-shape cutter, cut into hearts. Fill with Vanilla Buttercream, Classic Marshmallow Filling, or Homemade Marshmallow Crème. Cover with Sugar Glaze, decorate with large heart-shaped cake sprinkles, and let set. Pack in a box to give as a gift.

## Wedding Whoopies

Bake a batch of Mini Vanilla Whoopies. Fill with Vanilla Buttercream, Classic Marshmallow Filling, or Homemade Marshmallow Crème. Cover with white Sugar Glaze, add pink sugar flower cake decorations, and let set. If you want, spray with pink edible luster spray. Put in a dish to serve.

## Silver or Gold Anniversary Whoopies

Bake a batch of Mini Vanilla Whoopies. Fill with Vanilla Buttercream, Classic Marshmallow Filling, or Homemade Marshmallow Crème. Cover with white Sugar Glaze, add silver or gold dragees (cake decoration balls), and let set. If you want, spray with silver or gold edible luster spray. Put in a dish to serve.

## Baby Shower Whoopies

Bake a batch of Mini Vanilla Whoopies. Fill with Vanilla Buttercream, Classic Marshmallow Filling, or Homemade Marshmallow Crème. Cover half with pale pink and half with pale blue Sugar Glaze. Put a pink, blue, or white sugared almond on top of each and let set. Put in a dish to serve.

## Easter Whoopies

Bake a batch of Mini Chocolate Whoopies. Fill with Chocolate Buttercream. Cover with Chocolate Glaze, put a mini chocolate Easter egg on top of each, and let set. To serve, pile in a basket filled with tissue paper or shredded colored paper. Alternatively, don't frost the whoopies but add a mini chocolate Easter egg and wrap in colored foil. Hide in the backyard or house and have an Easter whoopie treasure hunt.

## Halloween Whoopies

Bake a batch of Pumpkin Whoopies (see page 44). Fill with orange Colored Buttercream. Cover with orange Colored Glaze and let set. Add a Halloween cake decoration to each before serving in a dish.

## Christmas Whoopies

Bake a batch of Mini Vanilla Whoopies. Fill with Vanilla Buttercream, Classic Marshmallow Filling, or Homemade Marshmallow Crème. Cut out star shapes from ready-to-use rolled white fondant to fit the tops of the whoopies. Place on top of each and decorate with silver or gold dragees (cake decoration balls). Pack into cellophane bags and tie with ribbon to give as gifts.

# Up-a-Notch Decorating Ideas

### For Adults & The Young at Heart

Bake a batch of Chocolate or Vanilla Whoopies. Fill with Buttercream and roll the sides in chopped pistachio nuts, slivered almonds, chopped pecans, chopped walnuts, or unsweetened cocoa.

Top with a piped swirl of Buttercream and add fresh fruit, such as a strawberry or raspberry, or a small chocolate.

### For Children

Bake a batch of Chocolate or Vanilla Whoopies, fill and then roll the sides in colorful mini candy-coated chocolates, chocolate chips, crushed candies, or cake-decorating sprinkles.

Top with a piped swirl shapes, or a candy.

### Marbled Whoopies

Make a batch of Chocolate and a batch of Vanilla Whoopie batter. Add the Vanilla Whoopie batter to the Chocolate Whoopie batter and, using a tablespoon, gently swirl the batters together to create a marbled effect. Don't overmix. Using a level 2-inch/5-cm ice-cream scoop or heaping tablespoon, put the batter onto parchment paper-lined baking sheets in 2-inch/5-cm diameter rounds about 1¼ inches/3 cm high, leaving at least 3 inches/7.5 cm between each round to allow room for spreading. Alternatively, put the batter in a greased whoopie pan. The mixture will make 24 whoopies. Fill with Chocolate or Vanilla Buttercream, or Homemade Marshmallow Crème or Chocolate Marshmallow Crème.

## Chocolate-Coated Whoopies

Make a batch of Chocolate Ganache. Take a filled Chocolate or Vanilla Whoopie or Mini Chocolate or Mini Vanilla Whoopie and dip half the whoopie in the warm Chocolate Ganache. Put on a wire rack, with a sheet of parchment paper or a tray under the rack to catch the drips, and let set.

## Black & White Whoopies

Bake a batch of Chocolate Whoopies and a batch of Vanilla Whoopies and match each "black" whoopie half with its closest "white" partner in size. This will make 24 whoopies. Fill with Chocolate or Vanilla Buttercream, or Homemade Marshmallow Crème or Chocolate Marshmallow Crème, or add a layer of both.

# Packaging & Presentation Ideas

The traditional way to wrap whoopies is in plastic wrap. This is not only a good way to store them but also makes them portable. They will keep like this at room temperature for up to three days.

To give as a gift, pack in cellophane bags, stacking them with a square of parchment paper between them to prevent them from sticking together. Tie with ribbon and add a tag.

Large whoopies can be arranged on a decorative plate and the whole thing wrapped in cellophane, tied with ribbon, and given as a gift along with the plate.

Pack Mini Whoopies in a single layer in an airtight container or box. If not frosted, they can be individually tied with thin ribbon to make them look attractive.

A gift of homemade whoopies is always appreciated, and packed in a stylish box, they will be especially welcomed. Sample templates are provided on the following pages. Line the box with tissue paper or parchment paper before filling with whoopies, placing parchment paper between them if stacking.

# A box for 1 whoopie

The template on this page for the box for a single whoopie can be photocopied at 200% scale. The other templates should be copied onto thin card using the measurements provided. To make the boxes, carefully cut as marked. Use a butter knife and a straightedge rule to score along the fold marks, then stick down the corners with a little white (PVA) glue, being careful not to let any glue get on to the exposed surfaces. Leave the glue to dry completely before you use the box.

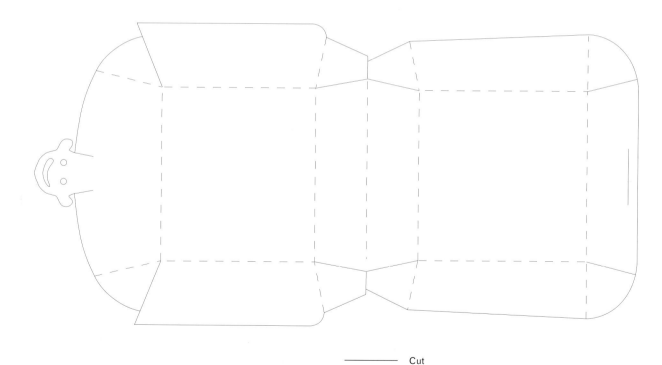

——————— Cut

— — — — Fold

## A box for 6 mini whoopies

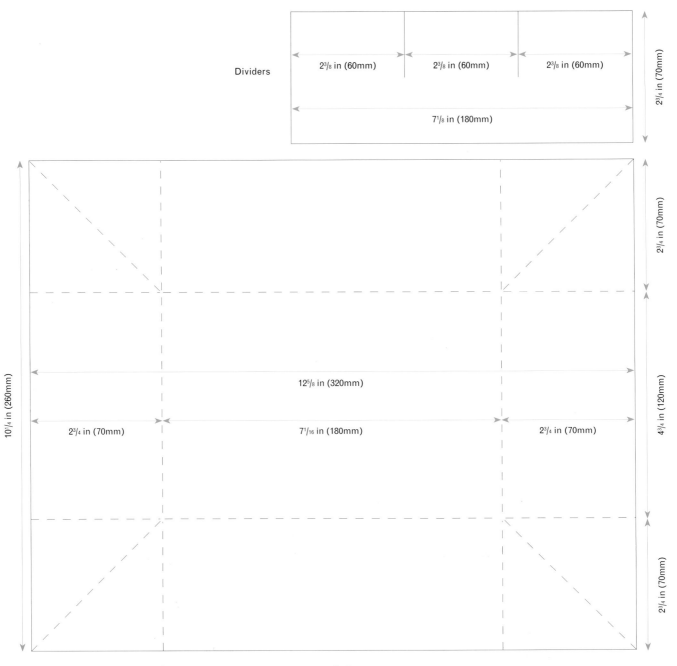

Dividers

2³/₈ in (60mm)  2³/₈ in (60mm)  2³/₈ in (60mm)

7¹/₈ in (180mm)

2³/₄ in (70mm)

2³/₄ in (70mm)

12⁵/₈ in (320mm)

4³/₄ in (120mm)

10¹/₄ in (260mm)

2³/₄ in (70mm)  7¹/₁₆ in (180mm)  2³/₄ in (70mm)

2³/₄ in (70mm)

Bottom

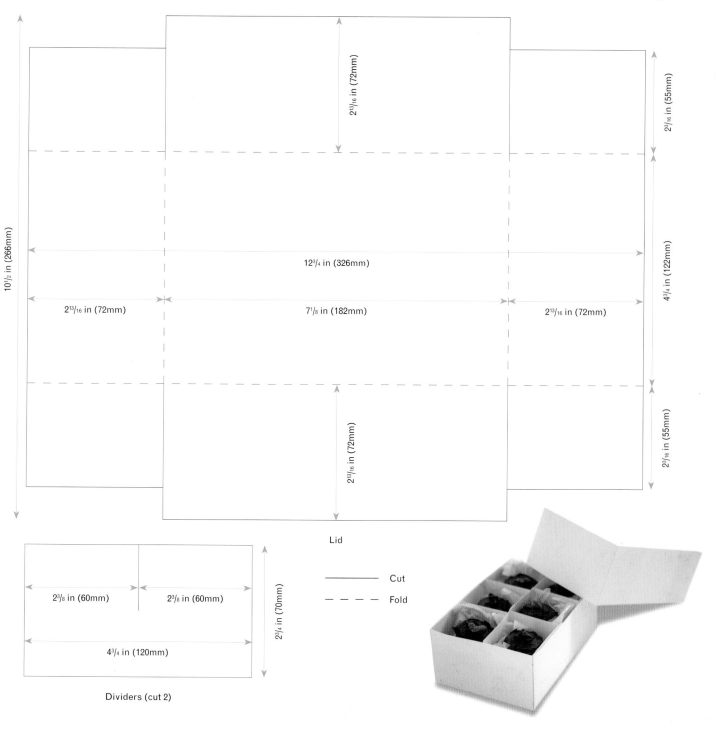

2<sup>13</sup>/₁₆ in (72mm)

2<sup>3</sup>/₁₆ in (55mm)

10<sup>1</sup>/₂ in (266mm)

12<sup>3</sup>/₄ in (326mm)

4<sup>3</sup>/₄ in (122mm)

2<sup>13</sup>/₁₆ in (72mm)

7<sup>1</sup>/₈ in (182mm)

2<sup>13</sup>/₁₆ in (72mm)

2<sup>3</sup>/₁₆ in (55mm)

2<sup>13</sup>/₁₆ in (72mm)

Lid

2<sup>3</sup>/₈ in (60mm)   2<sup>3</sup>/₈ in (60mm)

2<sup>3</sup>/₄ in (70mm)

4<sup>3</sup>/₄ in (120mm)

Dividers (cut 2)

————— Cut

— — — Fold

# A box for 4 whoopies

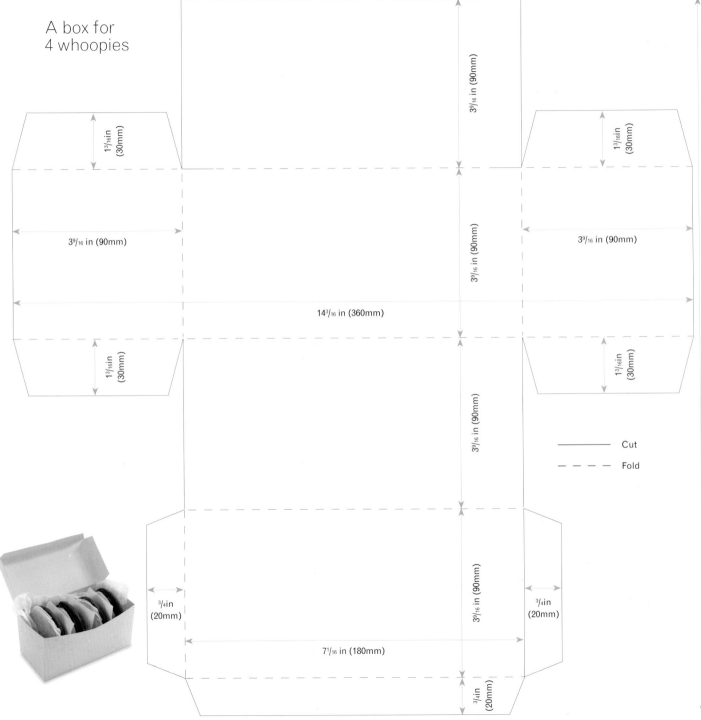

1³/₁₆ in (30mm)

3⁹/₁₆ in (90mm)

1³/₁₆ in (30mm)

1³/₁₆ in (30mm)

3⁹/₁₆ in (90mm)

3⁹/₁₆ in (90mm)

3⁹/₁₆ in (90mm)

3⁹/₁₆ in (90mm)

14³/₁₆ in (360mm)

1³/₁₆ in (30mm)

14¹⁵/₁₆ in (380mm)

3⁹/₁₆ in (90mm)

————— Cut

- - - - - Fold

³/₄ in (20mm)

3⁹/₁₆ in (90mm)

³/₄ in (20mm)

7¹/₁₆ in (180mm)

³/₄ in (20mm)

# Index

*Page references in bold refer to
where the recipe instructions appear*

10 9 8 7 6 5 4 3 2 1

Published by Sterling Publishing Co., Inc.
387 Park Avenue South, New York, NY 10016
Distributed in Canada by Sterling Publishing
c/o Canadian Manda Group
165 Dufferin Street
Toronto, Ontario, Canada M6K 3H6

Color origination by Ivy Press Reprographics

Printed and bound in China

Sterling ISBN: 978-1-4027-8647-1

For information about custom editions, special sales, premium
and corporate purchases, please contact Sterling Special Sales
Department at 800-805-5489 or specialsales@sterlingpublishing.com.

This book was conceived, designed, and produced by

**Ivy Press**
210 High Street, Lewes
East Sussex BN7 2NS, UK
www.ivy-group.co.uk

**Creative Director**  Peter Bridgewater
**Publisher**  Jason Hook
**Editorial Director**  Tom Kitch
**Senior Designer**  James Lawrence
**Designer**  Ginny Zeal
**Editor**  Jo Richardson
**Photographer**  Jeremy Hopley
**Stylist**  Susanna Tee

Acknowledgments
The publisher would like to thank the Steamer Trading Cookshop
(20/21 High Street, Lewes, UK) for providing the props for the
photoshoot, and iStockphoto/Kathleen Spencer for permission
to reproduce copyright material on page 67.